ANNIE

THE STORY OF AN APPLE

For Addison and Emmalynn ♡
follow your dreams!
☞
Joni Pfeiffer-Moser

By *Joni Pfeiffer - Moser*

Illustrated by : Janelle M. Hollis

~*~

Hallowed Abyss LTD

Story Author: Joan C. Pfeiffer-Moser
Original Illustrator: Janelle M. Hollis
Graphic Reconstruction Artist: Lénore M. Rhéaume

Published by Hallowed Abyss LTD
~Rhode Island~

For my beloved granddaughter,
Kristyn Louise Proctor,
whose love, inspiration and sense of wonder
helped bring Annie to fruition.

Annie the Apple, had a dream.

Ever since she was a tiny apple, Annie wanted to be a bright, beautiful apple sitting specially and serenely on a teacher's desk!

For Annie loved children, loved teachers, and Annie loved to learn.

Annie did not want to be an apple a day keeps the doctor away, and Annie did not want to be applesauce!

Annie knew that being a healthy apple for people to eat is a noble cause, but her dream was different.

Annie said, "I want to be an apple on a teacher's desk."

So, every sunny day, Annie faced the sun just a little to receive its warmth but was careful not to get burned!

When the wind blew, Annie held on very tightly so she wouldn't blow away or get shaken off the tree!

And, when it rained,

Annie let the warm rain bathe her shiny skin and drank

just enough water to keep her moist.

One day, it was time to be picked.

The pickers came and put Annie in a great big bushel basket. She was brought to a fruit stand where people buy apples to take them home.

The next day, Annie was in her basket resting comfortably when a very nice family picked up the basket, took it to the cash register, paid for it, and then put Annie and her basket carefully into the back of the car.

Annie was so excited !
The family had children and surely one of them
would want to take her to school to the teacher !
She held on tightly in the basket all the
way home.

Finally, they were home. The mom parked the car, and the children ran happily to the back of the car to get the basket of apples. "Careful, children," the dad scolded. "We want to make sure the apples aren't bruised or fall out of the basket. Both of you can take an apple to your teacher tomorrow!!." Annie glowed. Annie gleamed. Two children!! Two chances!! Surely one of them would pick her to take to the teacher tomorrow!!

As Annie and her basket were lifted from the car, Annie held on tightly for her basket ride to her new home.

The children laughed. Dogs barked in the distance.

Then, two dogs ran swiftly toward the family jumping joyfully.

"Down, Taffy, down!" We're bringing this basket of apples inside, and we have to be careful!"

Though the boy held on tightly, one dog jumped one more time.
Annie, one of the biggest and most beautiful apples, was on the top.
The dog's last jump gave the basket a jolt!

UP WENT ANNIE ! ! ! !

DOWN WENT ANNIE ! ! ! !

Down,
down,
down
on some
thick
green grass
on a hill.

She rolled,
and rolled,
and rolled
further and further away,
away from the children,
away from the family,
away from her new home.
And, most of all away from her
dream, her chance to be what she
always wanted to be--

A BIG, BRIGHT, BEAUTIFUL APPLE
ON A TEACHER'S DESK ! ! ! !

Other apples fell too, and the children quickly picked
them up. But Annie had rolled too far, and they did not see her.

Annie had rolled all the way down the hill to the side of the road.
Annie was bruised. Annie was hurt. Annie was very, very sad.
"Here I am lying by the the road ready to rot," she cried.
"Now I couldn't even be an apple a day keeps the doctor away or
even applesauce. And, I'll never have my dream come true to be a big,
bright, beautiful apple on a teacher's desk.
How can this happen to me?"

Soon, night came. It was the longest night of Annie's life.

Then, slowly but surely the sun came up, and a new day arrived.
Annie braced herself for a very sad day indeed where she would lie
by the side of the road and begin to rot.

Tears rolled down her cheeks bathing her bruise and shining her skin.

As the town woke up, Annie could hear the sounds

of cars rushing by, of dogs barking,

of children laughing and playing

as they walked along on their way to school.

SCHOOL ! ! **CHILDREN** ! !

Annie bravely gave the children her biggest, brightest, best smile !!!!!
"Maybe they will see me!" Patiently, she waited.
Annie, the Apple, was giving it one last try.
Children came, and children went.
Most of them had already walked by when she heard, "Look!
Look at that apple by the side of the road!
It is so big, so bright, and so beautiful!"

A boy gently picked up Annie and showed her to his friends.
He handed her to a girl. "We could eat it, " said the girl.
"We could take it home to make applesauce," said the boy.

"NO, LET'S TAKE HER TO SCHOOL AND GIVE HER TO THE TEACHER ! ! ! "

"TEACHER ! ! Did I hear TEACHER ? ! ! "

Annie was so excited. She puffed with pride, and her spirits soared as the children skipped happily to school.

And, as the teacher warmly held her and placed her gently on the desk,

Annie proudly smiled her biggest, beautiful smile!

For Annie's dream had come true.

Annie, the Apple, was a big, bright, beautiful apple sitting specially and serenely on a teacher's desk. For Annie loved children, loved teachers, and loved to learn.

Made in the USA
Middletown, DE
06 October 2017